MICHAEL RUBY

From an Album of Verses

SV
SurVision Books

First published in 2025 by
SurVision Books
Dublin, Ireland
Reggio di Calabria, Italy
www.survisionmagazine.com

Copyright © Michael Ruby, 2025

Design © SurVision Books, 2025

ISBN: 978-1-912963-59-1

This book is in copyright. No part of this publication may be reproduced, stored in a retrieval system, or transmitted in any form or by any means without the prior permission in writing from the publisher.

Acknowledgments

Grateful acknowledgment is made to the editors of the following, in which some of these poems, or versions of them, originally appeared:

Live Mag!: "Infinite consanguinity bears us"

Otoliths: "Master O master seated by the fire"

Unlikely Stories: "Tu ti spezzasti"

CONTENTS

"O lost in the gardens of this star"	5
"Tu ti spezzasti"	7
"Nothing to teach"	23
"Master O master seated by the fire"	25
"The cancellings, the negations are never final"	30
"You know then that it is not the reason that makes us happy or unhappy"	31
"You won't find peace in the country"	33
"Infinite consanguinity bears us"	34
"The far fields felt my heart"	36

"O lost in the gardens of this star"

> —Stéphane Mallarmé,
> translated by Robert T. S. Lowell

O lost, brother, beyond Alfred and filibustering
and Roberts and possum
and dimming and blossoming
parallelograms and happy hunting grounds
forked zone and sage delivery system
right without poignant

O lost, father, we went through the forms of hullabaloo
deepest disingenuous purebred etc.
together on the lank plastic basing
taken from buzzards and deregulated corners
holiday waiting

O lost, brother, registered and infiltrated
wonked within a happy meal of this peace in the Mideast,
    this peasant blouse in the hangnail
beyond housemates' puling
their holiday hoskered by round MacGuffins

O lost, brother, they took the sauce, the ready pell-mell
and honest-injun parallel bars
a tooth telltale for I don't know what persecution complex
ranked and polished, pre-regulated in the interest
of demonstrable poolroom and peacepipe
guaranteed song dodger, you know?

O lost, mother, whenever holiday onions strike
we went tethered to noodle pudding and the olive concoction
    and manufacturing process
the furthest along the time of rice procedures
together under a hollow-eyed hollow-tipped dugout
homilies and archery
we went telescoping Ungaretti into our closets
the furthest tommy gun since irregular Bilbao
together thick in the ring and piecemeal in the rising evidence
    of four-square vegetables

"Tu ti spezzasti"

—Giuseppe Ungaretti

I

Of all people perforated by health bars
eaten to prefabricate a justice system
bamboozled by an organized tooth fairy for our needs
    and holiday offering
the Rangoon Deli opens its horse works
tampers with college operating system playgrounds
telescopes to omnibus fealty a preset magnitude

Of all people the breathing incurs change machines and exact change
tollbooths chewed both ways for their annoying visits

Of all people in plastic hearth booths and old sewing factories
the onus on the inability to brigade through avenues of displaced

Of all people the breathing incurs the health bar
taking locks and ramming them to some conclusion
preset to our holiday information

Of all people most timely
organized through a watchword a handle a revealing pick
you see torsions peck in the holiday foxtrot
a random dispute over elegant timothies
pearly Dwight
divine sandwich shop a beacon

Of all people to pork this butcherblock basketball court
reassert the primacy of Virginia
signposts on the way to desert telepathy
quaking "destiny's journey"

Of all people the bronze demonstrates a healthy disrespect for
	breathing apparatus
a timebound element in the rising afflatus
all-day furniture and bog people
Tucson by nightfall broken for people to enter in a thousand places

Of all people the first to piece together
the imminent dissatisfaction
arm's length hollows to polish through the nose

Of all people reason coagulates and then separates into components
bland elements in a harmony
false teeth in the midst

Of all people the most true to rice
alcohol for logic and andirons to rest on the persuasive test
the murled orifice locked in disharmony
donnybrook and all
hollows and all
rising
setting
with exquisite what

Of all people phoned for his implacable defeats
regulated within an inch of his life
and then released to highway robbery
logistical perforation
runaway sign language in Gog or Oz
almost impregnable in right-of-way tolerance
legged out to all get-out
this go-by

Of all people farmed within liability
pried at surprisingly small cost

Of all people rock solid standard issue
registered so many times the pumice
the rice example and handbag discount
the total horizontal image tree
eaten through before the reading
lessened only by a layaway infrastructure
tilted onto a boys room tricycle factory
ominous in celebration

Of all people the possibility emerges and lingers there
this pointing neither one way nor another
within wraps very much within
and Puerto Rican and oiled to hopscotch
this berm so hard to understand for long
beneath our crops and repeal
teal leggings so duplicitous
the force needs a hemisphere for its oggles
to rasp and linger in the swelling
candystore's wee hours
when it's best to leave before testifying

Of all people so asked through to sponge
The right hospital without any fine tuning or ripple effect
Time for those crispy seas to leave their smorgasbord

Of all people the principle compromises
tasks for apple openings
regulate honest-to-goodness cipher
to empty the sorry sessions and pile on hoity-toity art things
you know you know how possible rivals answer the host
they polish their severance
toy an alligator
the icing

Of all people iron core
dogged for lopping

Of all people onioned in their gills
and sung to the house without disdain
soda for church and cyanide
for potatoes wouldn't sink to the level
required for onions oiled to the top

Of all people Jonah spake
baked tennis and forked Tabasco
termagant oats
smooth patterns
on imeing

II

In the world taste breaks a barrier
and synthesizes something originally outside itself
not Nuremburg or opera house pork
the Breckenridge of hopes and silver escalators
songbirds rotten in one insignificant part
hostage to unjustified fears
diming in the rising hindmost billboard
long sanctions and honest signpost to traces of—

In the world before wrong sounds and sights
feelings peeled and reasoned to an inch
breaks and the terrapin pelvis
for everyone to ground to powder
and then Rasputin the leggings

In the world prospered to a cryptic crisp
demonized for amusement's sake mostly
if a pullback materialized
if a rainmaker slipping in a drying puddle

In the world perforated by a beautiful doggone ice
pixilated within an inch of aromas
and shamelessly abandoned to rice
without pride of place or peals of time
to temporize the prime location
of this ironic placement
this disorganized incitement
to lock up the bestial silliness
and ring solvent upon solvent

in an effort to paralyze the psychology of a number
the racetrack in everyone's backyard
poised for greatness for so long
such a two-faced representative
of the fulfillment of our responsibilities
whatever they dredge from regions sublime and pricy
bathed in time solutions too speculative

III

I know oil brings this peace to our holiday
    I know toystores' teeth
I know thingumbob incunabula
    I know hapless pork and pontoon
I know hellebore raisins
    I know the suitcase for all wrongs
I know an olive toys with the angry patooties, and then, well, the
    registrar
    I know the sambulation pursues an ironclad fastening
I know the taint in the ample hawk
    I know how a cocoon can eat away at animals
I know the horror in the hambone, meal ticket and unstable dressing gown
    I know purple smears the tissues through a contraption
I know there was an egg inside a hollow
    I know beyond any possibility of samba
I know inside every box, inside the rightful

    I know saints persist to a pile
I know this perfect algorithm, this impregnable holiday from alligator
        keys
    I know the undersides of a shack
I know falsehood reigns more beautiful than truth, the unreal is infinite
        and the real finite
    I know after every rendition, interrogation
I know perfect peace reads the times of tomorrow to argue the Pete
        from its sinusitis eminence
    I know the world will take its oil
I know the perfect pure
    I know the song soars only to hightail into its suitcase
I know the sauce presents a reason to disabuse these heavens of their
        savor
    I know ranks prosecute teeth

I know this hurt seems to cringe
    I know segments pressurize and emulate the highway in certain
        neglected times
I know purely in the Rangoon of our hope
    I know for health to people purple

IV

I follow you without legislating rhyme or fillip
expressive beyond seminal Dunkin
And force field major ordure
I follow tandem butler and all-night soda
broken by a Caligula
I mean an irregular sandwich bar toystore idea
prosecuted and lumped into a red with Peggy
no no-no-no follow-up breasts
represent vesicles to prepare the dish
you know the tell
the soiled poice on the buggywhip
soup of every tetragrammaton
every which way the demon sandwich girl
boy to armies of holidays
and oilcans singing in their timing chase
so the tug pressed down on the orange
Tupperware of our baser designs

I follow you doorman
placeholder in the great game of chance
opening in the partition
the micturition
I follow you Rangoon poolhall
ice cream peace and Jesus
border tuna

I follow you for Pauline epistles
and irregular Samizdat
date certain
and ivy
geysers
no pellicle

I follow you
negotiated
with a perfect
and essential
clearinghouse
of
legislated annual
hunting grounds
you see sensors
table manners
escalate
this holiday
hophouse
and then where

I follow you huntsman
helmsman
singer of swifts
annual curtain
choice of
pelvic

I follow you most impressionistic
incapable of capturing

I follow you damaged beyond poyba
sluiced through
a talk
total
brainpan dynamo
all for time
to trike
alright
go play
homage
to the piece
eaten

I follow you
this oil in the gizzards
telephone
and popular solvent
in the event of
an ominous turn
in the belletrist
harmonica duct

I follow you Ritchie
how else can we see it
brace and cigar
silver offal
orange pileup

V

Once the kitchen crown sat unreachable
polished fort and all-night sing-along
the register in our proper boss and ring
found and delivered again
this time most hungry
most hungry of all
when eggs prime the sleep

Once the bishop points to all night
race into the Louis
same pockmark
same Bregman inside the elevator to ninepins

Once I led you horses to the deranged summit
Once I led you breaking the bone
Once I led you cold call and prepped
Once I led you through simoniac demons
sugars to hold the roofs and androids to prosper for
       an unspecified amount of time
all very commendable in its parking lot
only protected by a theory
(a principle to live by
a principle for someone else to live by
It's all so complicated, isn't it
the way we changed places
changed places again and again
each for our own very different reasons
That's the way people are
They do the same thing for different reasons)

Once I led you foster and polished
enjambed

Once I led you to the Pelham breezeway
officious and—
Once I led you poopy and hillbilly
ready range and helpful exchange
purse for salvation and syllables
unhealthy topic
Once I led you to the smokehouse
sweet water
milks
Once I led you poited for rice
and chocolate on the leg
Seminoles back after piece

*

Once I led you homogeneous and silver and olive and benefiting
 from a certain promiscuous pillbox

Once I led you through hallways to the ultimate prize
the disagreeable intransigent elephantine polished rooster of our
 hope for change
well you know what protocol passes for variety
the pool pooling benefits from a partial vibration of the tracheotomy
still bread and butter piecemeal tangent
legislature hophouse factory cigarette and all-night flow
...around hollow organs for oily rows to elephant pregnancies

Once I led you singing through the silver placemat
Once I led you to poil inside this smiling bime of our rickrack
on on going on without holiday sandwiches beef reek
becuz this is old as the hills and young as the soup
prime dicey eagle eye steambath ship

Once I led you through the solvent into the torrid pause of our elephants
they baked a special cream into vinegar and oiled the songbook
equated science and building and who in the end was qualified to
    disagree

Once I led you without polish or presence to arrogate belly
and Paul for rommon

Once I led you to reassess
the Bellin icicle time boy
Once I led you through force four
Pauline semicircle
nonfinite….

Once I led you talking of wholesome science brightness
fell alligator of our holiday workshop
Once I led you to practice an unsubstantiated
and they puked that vitamin
Once I led you breast and hearth bone sandwich
evil sign language languors for solvent hatchet songbird
pellicle of our soy braising devildogs
Once I led you for heaven knows seven or eleven
or reason beaten by bright hellebore
boiling inside all voice boxes
teaked to the dream Peabody sign language and one fine
    penitential pestilence

Once I led you to the sink of this disinfectant
relishing a heavy hungry insoluble comic
a pause in the basketball
and without an opposite field
a posture so breathed and fibbed
porked and alighted
sign language and hunger in Hungary
the end that wasn't the end
a time sale penchant for registered apples and lemons

Once I led you to gates written with purple right and onion
a long alligator in her heart of hearts
fell rest stops ransomed for a balk a dog

VI

You belly to the suitcase and throw off a thousand
inside the first Thanksgiving of our foresight
inside the lackluster target
the insurmountable incremental

You furrow
and egg on the pirates

You really can't answer the ribbon
the riboflavin
of a heartbeat
and the tasteless representation

Your right cheekbone objects
the password has been stolen and passed around
all out there

You blank the hill town
and prestidigitate until the once and future sandwich shop flexes its
 muscles
and changes the government of the safe haven
this eggshell this hysteria
on top of a hand grenade for healthy teeth

*

You cry from a particular bone above the eyes
the horn to its conclusion
the birds prepped for a distinction
cosmopolitan in its hankering for that easternmost place
the signs running through numbers
answering these pincushions
with a roundabout
roustabout
most ingenious combination
of salt and sugar
sugar and salt

You cry an infinitesimal house
ice on irregular torches
Hellgate inside the Pleasant Valley Sunday
of our omnibus fears and hopes
carefully packaged throughout the rind and insinuated into
 the national psyche
  a pioneer in the precise region

You cry throughout the open passage
the region lying underneath
the polygon inside the box
the Monmouth self-protection league
every racket a fragment of the great crime

You cry the filters predate this underwater Orange Revolution
held together by rubber and an ominous substitute for leather
the Holy Grail, the onetime Holy Grail in this distribution

"Nothing to teach"

> "There was no need for speech
> and nothing to teach"
> —Osip Mandelstam,
> translated by Robert Tracy

I

An old-fashioned razor lives in the closet
Among the sorry icicles of Danang

For every signpost a rock
A rocker to hollow the blank operation
A boy ambushed the settled piano
You embody Douglas and Pete
Not candy nor pregnancy nor Halloween
Not living nor dying, nor anything else

Danang knew the escape route
A household in the middle of the moon
A pirate in the pink pillbox
Inside every jackhammer
And jackdog, alone in the alibi

I tried to open the highway jar
Already drank the green potion
Already lacquered the handlebars
Rounded up Tobias and the holiday troop
Weathering no more the answer

II

Rags for wisdom and songbooks
For lease on the way to South Sawmill
Under the junction of performance status
Hostile time for possible socks
Seeming breathing apparatus
Alone among the mullah sightings
Time in an impossible automobile

To find high signs of dispute
A ragged disregard for everything sacred

No infinite inferior potsherd
To broil in the midnight moon of Ool
Dangblasted and seasoned to perfection
Before rhyming sizes an orangutan
And orange juice in professions of faith

No hazardous materials on the journey
Long I-beams to bake the cake
Becalmed policy for rongommons
That simple and that complex

The race plays on emotions
Ranging from messenger to iodine
In the freedom to paralyze this parallelogram
Hope the fence of tolerable bandages
And pocket the bombast rocket

"Master O master seated by the fire"

—Wallace Stevens

I

Master oleaginous
O master parallax
Seated four-square
By the fire of our squall

Master powderpuff
O master houseguest
Seated alligators
By the fire hobbled

II

Master
We didn't
Wrong the patooties

Master
Arm's length
Isn't enough

Master
Open season
On falafel

Master
We never tire
Of your
Hullaballoo
Your
Control climate

Master
Throngs
Smell
This
Polished
Sandal

Master
Fortune
Smiles on
Sausages

Master
If doilies
Can't
Impregnate
Porches

Master
Free
With
Power
Possibility
Free
With
Our
Holiday
And
All-night
Sandwich

Master
Free with our
Televisions
Sizzling
To no end

Master
Free with our
Implications
And tethers

Master
Free with our
Umbrage
And
Phone
Personality

Master
Free with our
Ontology
Our
Hysterectomy

Master
Free with our
Understanding
Our
Pelvic bone

Master
Free with our
Undulation
Our
Incrustation

Master
Free with our
Humbug
Our
Paralysis
Our
Persuasion

III

Master Olmec
O master polygon
Seated bouillabaisse
By the fire destined

Master stratus
O master paragon
Seated pork
By the fire frustrated

Master operagoer
O master placemark
Seated hoplites
By the fire warden

Master committeeman
O master pointillist
Seated northward
By the fire Risperdal

Master locksmith
O master tailgate
Seated ominously
By the fire elephantine

Master register
O master peashooter
Seated effectually
By the fire brilliantined

"The cancellings, the negations are never final"

—Wallace Stevens

To fulfil
This denomination

They rise above us
Infinitesimal
Positive vibrations

Our responsibility
Hooked and eaten
Without regard

For the salvageable
Procedure to dunk
Underrepresented
In this fine
This parallel
This legislated
This Egremont
This household name
This all-night
This boat place

They are not
They will not be
Only we are
We will be

"You know then that it is not the reason that makes us happy or unhappy"

—Wallace Stevens

You know then the inside will never present

You know then ice cream augurs a succession of elephantine proportions
You know then without any indication of sustenance
Without the rongommon in the purple ice capades, the transubstantial

It is not the reason to imply a fall
It is not the reason a flame fails to ignite a wall
It is not the reason for eggs or orderlies

It is not the reason to place, to register, to pacify, to incubate,
    to intubate

That makes us possible before impossible, remote before proximate

That makes us without any information

Happy or unhappy in the green snake
Happy or unhappy in the Rosenbaum
Happy or unhappy about the power saw
Death has its beginnings in many places
Life has its beginnings in many places

Happy or unhappy in this sidereal sideshow, this bulldozer of breath
Far-fetched, implemental

Happy or unhappy to place our confidence in the confidence man
Happy or unhappy about Tabasco
Happy or unhappy about all the turns in a road
Happy or unhappy above the boiler room and boys room

"You won't find peace in the country"

—William Carlos Williams

You won't find an elevator in the foul pole
or a rocky pomegranate
or a knowledgeable sauceboat

Peace! slightly gameshows
Peace! rocking pocketbook

In the country of preeminent masking
and pear backing
and the operation of points

You won't find the Tabasco in the sign language
or mace for support
or the answer to hormones

"Infinite consanguinity bears us"

—Hart Crane

Monsoons take us home
To Monzon on Wide World of Sports
For the reckoning and answer

Hope of ether
And old time doggone

Force fields of sanity
And longtime implicated
Eaten holistically
Breadbasket of panjandrum

We leave peopled for residence
Leave them the sausage positives
There Rangooned
Who hula'd
Hellbent on pork bellies
And isolated solvents
In this our unspecific

Yes to all of the above sandwiches
So it is the rice of acknowledgeable Cincinnati

Yes to all of the above sandwiches
So it is in the infomercial of our daisies
So it is without the thick walls of finance

So it is... pearly and soft
Frank in the form of pellicles
So it is teething holiday sandwiches
Draking on the hustings
And otherwise polishing the rightful barbershop
In this on and off again (sizing arena, right?)
So it is
So it is
Yes to all of the Telemann for your habits
Yes to all of the Rosencrantz with a cigar

"The far fields melt my heart"

—Sylvia Plath

I'm not going to know
The tool will presume
Peace singes the offing

It's time
In the dog shop
The chaperone pastes
One-hundred dollar bills
The ice exaggerates

We have them
Innocuous thunder
Noxious jet, do not melt my heart

We never have them
There in the improbable
Hospitalized or not
Among dingdongs
Filibustering with the rest
Punting again

I know they are greener pastures
Sample pells
Lemon regulars
In the ice cream of our eggshells

I'm not going
On the onion
Inside the sockdolager (whatever that is)

I'm not going
Before fashion porks the twofold being and bistro
The prime manumission in this spaceship
Lost to lesser segments
And eaten to—

It's time and might be right
I know that within each egg
Inside the floorboards
Welcome to ringing sizes
I know the best information often rises before it falls

Selected Poetry Titles Published by SurVision Books

Contemporary Tangential Surrealist Poetry: An Anthology
Edited by Tony Kitt
ISBN 978-1-912963-44-7

Noelle Kocot. *Humanity*
(New Poetics: USA)
ISBN 978-1-9995903-0-7

Mikko Harvey & Jake Bauer. *Idaho Falls*
(Winner of James Tate Poetry Prize 2018)
ISBN 978-1-912963-02-7

John Bradley. *Spontaneous Mummification*
(Winner of James Tate Poetry Prize 2019)
ISBN 978-1-912963-13-3

Charles Kell. *Pierre Mask*
(Winner of James Tate Poetry Prize 2019)
ISBN 978-1-912963-19-5

Charles Borkhuis. *Spontaneous Combustion*
(Winner of James Tate Poetry Prize 2021)
ISBN 978-1-912963-30-0

Noah Falck and Matt McBride. *Prerecorded Weather*
(Winner of James Tate Poetry Prize 2022)
ISBN 978-1-912963-39-3

George Kalamaras. *Through the Silk-Heavy Rains*
ISBN 978-1-912963-28-7

Order our books from http://survisionmagazine.com

www.ingramcontent.com/pod-product-compliance
Lightning Source LLC
Chambersburg PA
CBHW061312040426
42444CB00010B/2607